Solids, Liquids, and Gases

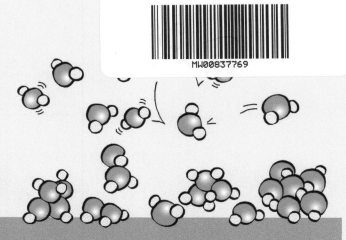

Illustrations: Janet Moneymaker
Design/Editing: Marjie Bassler

Solids, Liquids, and Gases
ISBN 978-1-953542-06-9

Published by Gravitas Publications Inc.
www.gravitaspublications.com
www.realscience4kids.com

Imagine that you could travel inside an ice cube.

What would happen if
the ice started to melt?

Some of the water can also float into the air.

Water exists in three states.

These three states are

solid, liquid, and **gas.**

Water in the air is a **gas** called **water vapor**.

Ice is water as a **solid**.

Water can be a **liquid**.

Water is made of **molecules.**

Molecules are made of **atoms.**

Am I made of molecules too?

Yes.

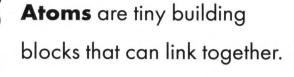

Atoms are tiny building blocks that can link together.

Atoms make up everything we touch, taste, smell, and see.

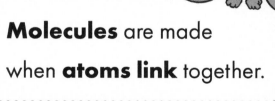

Molecules are made when **atoms link** together.

Water molecules have **energy** and can move.

I have energy and I can move!

Energy is needed to do **work.**

Work happens when a **force** moves an object.

Force is any action that changes...
...the **location** of an object,
...the **shape** of an object,
...**how fast or how slowly** an object is moving. (This is called the **speed** of an object.)

Water molecules in ice have low energy.

These molecules do not move very much.

When I have low energy, I sit.

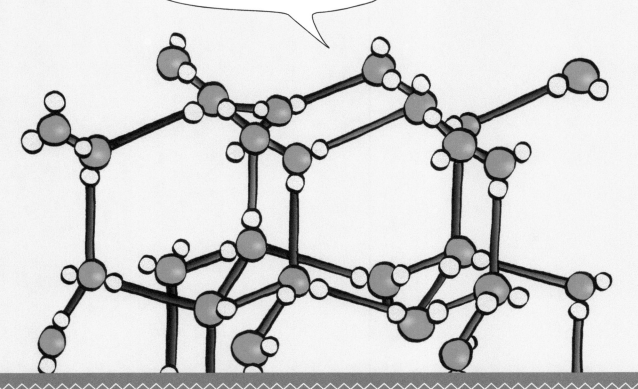

The molecules in liquid water have more energy and start to bounce around.

When I have more energy, I walk.

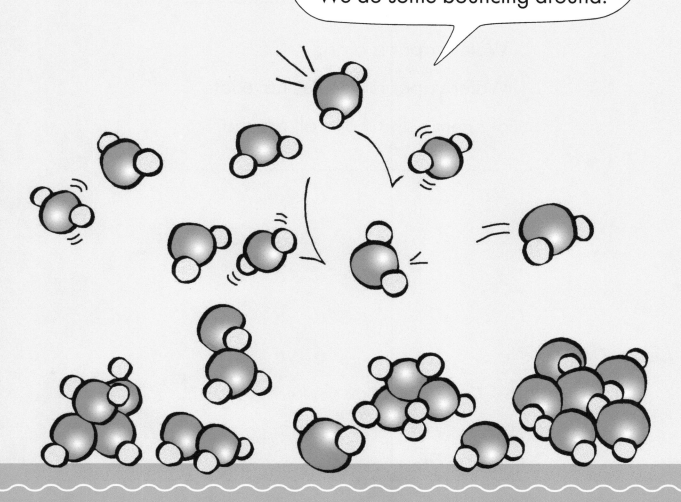

Water vapor is a gas.

Water vapor molecules have lots

of energy and move all around.

When I have lots of energy, I run!

The only difference between water as ice, water as liquid, and water as gas is how much energy the molecules have.

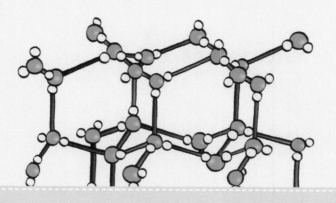

Water with low energy is a solid.

Water with more energy is a liquid.

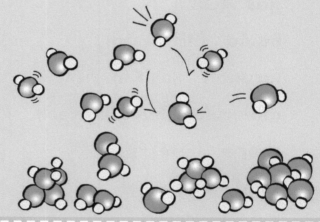

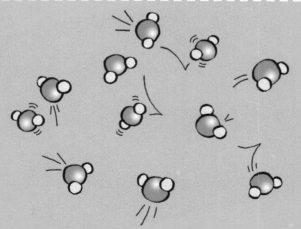

Water with lots of energy is a gas.

How to say science words

atom (AA-tum)

energy (E-nuhr-jee)

force (FAWRSS)

gas (GAS)

liquid (LIH-kwuhd)

location (loh-KAY-shun)

molecule (MAH-lih-kyool)

shape (SHAYP)

solid (SAH-luhd)

speed (SPEED)

state (STAYT)

water (WA-tuhr)

water vapor (WA-tuhr VAY-puhr)

work (WERK)

What questions do you have about
SOLIDS, LIQUIDS, AND GASES?

Learn More Real Science!

Complete science curricula from Real Science-4-Kids

Focus On Series

Unit study for elementary and middle school levels

Chemistry
Biology
Physics
Geology
Astronomy

Exploring Science Series

Graded series for levels K–8. Each book contains 4 chapters of:

Chemistry
Biology
Physics
Geology
Astronomy

Printed in the USA
CPSIA information can be obtained
at www.ICGtesting.com
LVHW070917230823
755951LV00032B/676